AGAINST ALL ODDS

David Clayton

OXFORD

UNIVERSITY PRESS

OXFORD
UNIVERSITY PRESS

is a department of the University of Oxford.
It furthers the University's objective of excellence in research, scholarship,
and education by publishing worldwide in

Oxford   New York
Auckland   Cape Town   Dar es Salaam   Hong Kong   Karachi
Kuala Lumpur   Madrid   Melbourne   Mexico City   Nairobi
New Delhi   Shanghai   Taipei   Toronto

With offices in

Argentina   Austria   Brazil   Chile   Czech Republic   France   Greece
Guatemala   Hungary   Italy   Japan   Poland   Portugal   Singapore
South Korea   Switzerland   Thailand   Turkey   Ukraine   Vietnam

Oxford is a registered trade mark of Oxford University Press
in the UK and in certain other countries

British Library Cataloguing in Publication Data

Data available

ISBN: 978-0-19-846132-6

5 7 9 10 8 6 4

Printed in China by Imago

Paper used in the production of this book is a natural,
recyclable product made from wood grown in sustainable forests.
The manufacturing process conforms to the environmental
regulations of the country of origin.

Acknowledgements

The publisher would like to thank the following for permission to reproduce photographs: **p4** Hearts Football Club,
p5 Science & Society Picture Library, **p6** Getty Images/AFP, **p7** Getty Images/AFP, **p8** Getty Images News, **p9** Getty
Images/Hulton Archive, **p10** Empics, **p11** Topfoto, **p12**t Noah Hamilton, b Getty Images/Photographers Choice,
p13b Empics, **p14** Getty Images/Robert Harding World Imagery, **p15** Geoff Bell, **p16** Empics, **p17** Empics, **p18**
Getty Images/Photographers Choice, **p19**t Empics, **p19**b Empics, **p20** Getty Images Sport, **p21**l Sporting Heroes,
p21r Empics, **p22** Empics, **p23** Empics

Cover: Topfoto/Topham/PA

Illustrations by Mark Duffin: **p6**, **p8**, **p11**, **p14**, **p23**; David McAllister/NB illstration Limited **p5**

Designed by Bigtop

Contents

Where there are people, there is sport

Introduction

One of the great things about sport is that you never know what you can do until you try. Some people beat illness, injury or accidents to compete. Others keep on trying until they succeed. Finally, there are those who achieve things that seem impossible. All these are part of sport and the joy of 'winning against all odds'.

People play sport in all sorts of places. Our first example of 'winning against all odds' has a surprising setting.

Football in No-Man's-Land – Christmas 1914

In 1914, thousands of soldiers fought in World War One in France. Many of the soldiers were sportsmen who fought with their friends in **Pals' battalions**. The whole of the Hearts football team from Edinburgh went to France together as soldiers in this way.

The Hearts in France.

The soldiers faced their enemies in two lines of trenches. Trenches were a series of ditches, hundreds of kilometres long. The war was fought in 'No-Man's-Land', a gap of a few hundred metres between the two lines.

The enemy soldiers met on Christmas Day. Footballers began to play.

On Christmas Day 1914, something amazing happened. Near **Armentières** in France, soldiers sang and shouted across to their enemies.

Then they went out into 'No-Man's-Land' and no one was shot.

Footballs were produced. Coats were put down and used as goal posts. There were many games that day. For one day, sport had taken the place of war.

Lance Armstrong's 'Perfect seven'

The Tour de France

The Tour de France is the hardest cycle race in the world. Every summer, the best cyclists in the world race each other. They race for more than 20 days through the southern sun, the northern rain and the mountain snow.

N
W — E
S

— Race sections
— Plane connection
— Train connection

Paris
(the finish)

Strasbourg
(the start)

Alps

Pyrenees

The Tour de France is made up of various stages which together make up 3000–4000 km. Riders sometimes travel to the next stage by plane or train.

Riders come down mountains at over 100 kilometres per hour – the speed of a car on a motorway. Riders crash every year; some even die.

The 2006 tour. The route changes every year.

'Perfect seven'

In 1996 Lance Armstrong of the USA was seriously ill with cancer. He had only four chances in ten of getting better, but he did.

Three years later, he was the best rider in the world again and went on to win the Tour de France seven times in seven years.

Armstrong's Tour de France wins

Year	Time (distance varies)	Average speed	Winning margin
1999	91 hr 32 min 16 sec	40.273 kph	7 min 37 sec
2000	92 hr 33 min 8 sec	38.57 kph	6 min 2 sec
2001	86 hr 17 min 28 sec	40.02 kph	6 min 44 sec
2002	82 hr 5 min 12 sec	39.93 kph	7 min 17 sec
2003	83 hr 41 min 12 sec	40.940 kph	1 min 1 sec
2004	83 hr 36 min 2 sec	40.553 kph	6 min 19 sec
2005	88 hr 15 min 2 sec	41.654 kph	4 min 40 sec

How did Armstrong do it?

He has a slow **resting heartbeat**.

He can ride mountains well.

He can ride short **time trials** well.

He has faster leg speed than most cyclists.

He has a good support team.

He has courage.

Lance Armstrong in the lead.

David Walliams and the Channel challenge

Swimming the English Channel is one of the greatest feats in the world. More people have climbed Everest than have been able to swim across the Channel. Swimming in this cold (15° Celsius) 35-kilometre stretch of water is made more dangerous by the many huge tankers and other vessels that cross it. Stinging jellyfish also make the swim very difficult.

However, David Walliams, comedy star of the TV show *Little Britain*, crossed it on 4 July 2006 in 10 hours 30 minutes. This is one of the 50 fastest times for the swim.

Walliams covered his body in grease to help keep warm during the crossing.

STARTS 5.30am
Shakespeare
Beach

Dover

England

English Channel

Calais

FINISHES 4.00pm
(approx)
Cap Gris-Nez

Boulogne

France

Walliams was not an experienced swimmer, but he trained for eleven months for the event. He raised money for the charity Sport Relief to help children in poor countries.

The route taken by David Walliams.

We can see how well Walliams did when we look at the times other Channel swimmers achieved. Only 10 per cent of those who attempt it succeed.

English Channel record-breakers

Record fastest swim	Swimmer	Time	Year
by a man	Christof Wandrastch	7 hr 3 min 52 sec	1980
by a woman	Penny Lee Dean	7 hr 40 min	1978
Youngest boy (aged 11 years 11 months)	Thomas Gregory	11 hr 54 min	1988
Youngest girl (aged 12 years 118 days)	Samantha Druce	15 hr 28 min	1983
Oldest man (aged 70 years 4 days)	George Burnstad	15 hr 59 min	2004
Oldest woman (aged 57 years)	Carol Sing	12 hr 32 min	1999

First timer

The first to swim the English Channel was Captain Matthew Webb in 21 hours 45 minutes in 1875. He later drowned swimming across the Niagara Rapids in America.

Sheer luck!

Sometimes people take a chance and win when they should lose.

Joe Gaetjens, the scorer for USA.

Football

In 1950, England had the best football team in the world. The USA had hardly ever won a game at all. However, in the 1950 World Cup, the USA beat England 1–0. England missed more than ten chances to score. The USA had one header and won. Sheer luck!

Horse racing

In the 1967 **Grand National**, a horse called Foinavon had odds of 100–1 against him winning. He was a good horse but often fell.

In the race, he started slowly. Most of the other horses were in front of him. Then there was a great fall. Horses got in each other's way, but lucky Foinavon got through and went on to win. The disastrous fence at the famous Aintree course is named after him now.

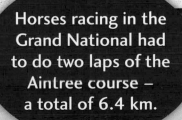

Horses racing in the Grand National had to do two laps of the Aintree course – a total of 6.4 km.

Even sharks can't stop her – Bethany Hamilton

Bethany Hamilton learned how to **surf** when she was five years old. By the age of 11, she was a champion surfer in Hawaii.

Shark attack

However a 4-metre-long tiger shark bit off Hamilton's left arm when she was surfing at the age of 13. She swam ashore. Even though she had lost a lot of blood, hospital staff managed to save her life.

Bethany Hamilton before the accident.

Teeth like these took off Bethany's arm with one bite.

Fighting back

Ten weeks after the shark attack, she was surfing again. Less than two years later, in 2005, she was fifth in a big surfing event. In 2006, she won a gold medal with the Hawaii team in the World Junior Surfing Championships.

Bethany, back on her board in 2004.

Bethany showed what could be done with determination and courage.

Bethany Hamilton – 2006 World Surfing Champion.

Try, try and try again – Mike Cudahy

Not many people can run a marathon. A marathon is 42.195 kilometres and is usually run on flat roads. Imagine running ten marathons over hills, through mud and along dirt tracks, all within three days.

The Pennine Way is not an easy place to run.

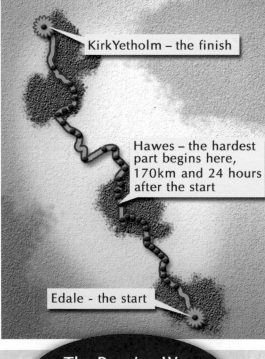

KirkYetholm – the finish

Hawes – the hardest part begins here, 170km and 24 hours after the start

Edale - the start

The Pennine Way race, usually runs South to North.

The Pennine Way

The Pennine Way is more than ten marathons in length. It is 434 kilometres of hills, swamps and moors, between Edale in England and Kirk Yeltholm in Scotland. Between 1980 and 1984, Mike Cudahy of England made several attempts to run it. Seven times, he had to give up. Finally, at the eighth attempt, he succeeded.

The hard, hard hills

In the Pennines, there can be hot sunshine, rain and even snow in summer. If you want to run the Pennine Way in three days, there is no time for sleep. You run night and day.

Mike Cudahy ran 200 kilometres a week when training. He was super fit, yet, even so, you can see in the table below what the wild hills did to him before he beat them!

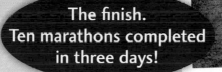

The finish.
Ten marathons completed
in three days!

Mike Cudahy's attempts

Year	Got as far as ...	Distance	Reason for failure
1980	Cowling	100 km	Big storm, high winds, injured leg
1980	Hawes	170 km	Feet cut to pieces, felt like "shoes full of glass". Rainstorm in dark
1981	Hawes	170 km	Fell over wood in swamp, damaged leg
1981	Dufton	260 km	Very dark night, hot day, feet in great pain, slowed in heat
1982	Dufton	260 km	Too hot, knew he could make it but feet failed him. Mike said, "Never again!"
1983	Dufton (ran from north-south)	160 km	Snowstorm, risk of death from cold
1984	Hardraw	175 km	Bone-hard ground, hot and dry, legs too stiff to move. Could not even walk
1984	Kirk Yelthom	430 km	Did it! Finished in 2 days 21 hours 54 minutes and 30 seconds

'One day I'll do it!' – Kelly Holmes

Junior star

Kelly Holmes was always a good runner. When she was 13 years old, she won an English Schools' title. When she was 23, she was the National 800 metre Champion.

Top runners train hard. Holmes trained very hard – perhaps too hard.

The highs and lows of Kelly Holmes' career

1996 (26 years old): 4th in the Olympic 800 m, but ran in pain – she had run with a broken leg!

1999 (29 years old): hurt her leg in the World Championships and could hardly run

2000 (30 years old): although ill, finished 3rd in the Olympic 800 m

2002 (32 years old): finished 3rd in the European 800 m and won the 1500 m in the Commonwealth Games in Manchester

Hurt again

In 2003, aged 33, after coming second in the World Championship 800 metres in Paris, she was hurt again. But somehow she got to the 2004 **Olympics** injury-free. At the 2004 Olympics, in **Athens**, she won two gold medals – in the 800 and 1500 metre races.

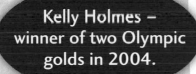

Kelly Holmes – winner of two Olympic golds in 2004.

British women winners of Olympic gold medals in athletics

Winner	Year	Athletics event
Mary Rand	1964	Long jump
Ann Packer	1964	800 m
Mary Peters	1972	**Pentathlon**
Tessa Sanderson	1984	Javelin
Sally Gunnell	1992	400 m Hurdles
Denise Lewis	2000	**Heptathlon**
Kelly Holmes	2004	800 m and 1500 m

Kelly Holmes became one of the few British women to have won an Olympic gold medal in **athletics**.

Beyond impossible – Reinhold Messner

The greatest

Reinhold Messner is the most famous climber in the world. He has done things that other climbers thought impossible. He is a man who achieves the seemingly impossible.

Everest

This is Everest, the highest mountain in the world at 8850 metres.

When people climb Everest, they usually employ people called porters to set up camps higher up the mountain. Other porters carry **oxygen** for them. In spite of this help, over 140 climbers have died on the mountain.

Messner climbed Everest on his own. He carried his own tent and did not use oxygen. People said that he was crazy, but he did it. He is a strong man.

Messner climbed all the world's mountains that are over 8000 metres high – without oxygen. He climbed these peaks between 1970 and 1986. His 'impossible' solo Everest climb was in 1980. Afterwards, he needed more challenges.

The South Pole

Messner decided to walk across the Antarctic via the South Pole in 1989. He did it with Arved Fuchs. They completed the 2,500 kilometre expedition in 92 days, each pulling his own sledge without the use of dogs.

Later, in 2000, Messner returned to the Antarctic to climb across the icy mountains of South Georgia with other climbers.

She didn't give up – Mary Peters

Mary Peters was a top Irish athlete. Everybody liked her, but few thought she had a chance of winning a gold medal at the 1972 Olympics.

In 1972, she was aged 33 and ranked only fifth-best in the world at the **pentathlon**. In her hometown of Belfast, she trained on a poor track, but for six weeks just before the Olympics she got the chance to train in America.

Peters at the start of the 1972 Olympic pentathlon 200 m – the race of her life.

World record, Olympic champion

At the Olympics in **Munich**, Mary Peters led in the pentathlon after a first day of good marks in the hurdles, high jump and shot put. However, on the second day, Heidi Rosendahl, the German star, almost broke the long jump world record. It was all down to the final event, the 200 metres.

Years before, Peters had failed in a final event. The memory of this was probably in Peters' mind. At 33 years of age, Peters now had to beat her lifetime best to win.

In the final, Rosendahl raced ahead but Peters didn't give up. She stormed home in 24.08 seconds to win *and* she broke the world record!

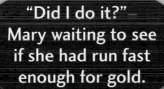

"Did I do it?" – Mary waiting to see if she had run fast enough for gold.

"Yes!" – record-breaker and Olympic champion!

The amazing Jane Tomlinson

Until 1990, Jane Tomlinson was a person leading an ordinary life. Then, one day, she found out that she had a serious illness – cancer. Although she fought against it, she did not get better. By 2000, the news was very bad. Doctors told her that she had little time to live.

Tomlinson decided to do some amazing things, despite the fact that she was very ill.

Jane Tomlinson running in the New York Marathon in 2005.

Athlete!

Tomlinson:
- ran the London Marathon three times
- ran the New York Marathon
- cycled the length of Britain
- cycled from Leeds to Rome
- completed the **Ironman triathlon**.

All this is was done to raise money for charities such as Macmillan Cancer Relief, The Paediatric Acute Services in Leeds, and the Damon Runyon Cancer Research Foundation in the USA.

Then, in 2006, Jane Tomlinson took part in her biggest fundraising challenge – to cycle 6780 kilometres across America. She started on Thursday, 29 June and completed the amazing feat on Friday, 1 September.

Tomlinson's ride across America raised money for UK and US based cancer and children's charities.

Start
San Francisco

Finish
New York

Main stopping points

The ride took 65 days.

She has raised millions for others.
Her courage has been truly extraordinary.

Glossary

Armentières a French town 50 km from the English Channel

Athens a city in Greece where the Olympics were held in 2004

athletics sports activities such as running, jumping and throwing a javelin or shot put

Grand National a horse race with big jumps (fences), held in Liverpool

heptathlon a competition involving seven events: 100 m hurdles, high jump, shot put, 200 m run, long jump, javelin throw, 800 m run

Ironman triathlon race that involves: swimming (3.86 km), cycling (180.2 km), followed by a marathon run (42.2 km).
It is the hardest race in the world

Munich a city in Germany where the Olympics were held in 1972

Olympics a world championship held every four years

oxygen a gas in the air that we need to breathe to live. Many mountaineers breathe oxygen from tanks because there is little air on high mountains

Pals' battalion an army group of up to a thousand men from the same town or who work for the same company

parachute sails kind of parachute-shaped kites used to pull things along

pentathlon a competition involving five events: hurdles, shot-put, high jump, long jump, 200 m run

resting heartbeat the number of times the heart beats in one minute when the person is resting

surfing riding rough waves on a special board called a surfboard. 'Surf' is the word for the rough waves themselves

time trials races against the clock. In a time trial, riders take turns to ride and their time is recorded